Essential Question
What happens when families work together?

Families at Work

by Ann Weil

CHAPTER 1

Families Work Together

Brothers and sisters help keep their home clean.

Families work together in many ways. Parents want their children to help out at home. When families work together at home, chores can get done quickly.

There are many jobs kids can do at home. They can set the table for meals and help with the dishes afterward. They can help clean up the house. They can take out the trash. Some kids work at jobs outside their homes, too. Child **actors** work in movies and on TV shows. Some of them even become famous!

Some kids deliver newspapers.

It is not easy to become an actor. But there are many other kinds of jobs kids can do to make money. Kids can sell lemonade and baked goods in their neighborhood. Kids can babysit, walk dogs, or mow lawns. These are all ways kids can work to make money.

Some kids save the money they make for the future. Others spend the money they make on things they want or need now. Sometimes kids use the money they earn to help pay for things their family can enjoy together.

3

In some jobs, kids wear a uniform or badge.

Parents help their children with their jobs. Together, they might discuss which jobs would fit into their family's **schedule**. Parents also help their children find and apply for some jobs. Kids may need their parents to drive them to work.

When You're Older...

Some places teens can work:

- > an office
- > a store
- > a movie theater
- > a baseball park

CHAPTER 2

A Lemonade Stand

You may have most of what you need to sell lemonade at home.

Selling lemonade from a homemade stand is a common tradition in America. It's also a fun way for families to work together. There's something for everyone in the family to do. Even the youngest family members can join in.

The recipe for lemonade is simple. Lemon juice, water, and a sweetener are all you need. The lemonade stand also needs a sign. Making the sign can be a fun project for young artists. The sign should tell the cost of the lemonade so customers know how much to pay.

Parents and grandparents can use tools to make the stand. Kids can help, too. If there's no **handyperson** in the family, a folding table with a tablecloth can work well.

It is important to choose the right time and place to sell lemonade. People like lemonade on hot, sunny days. Also, more people are out enjoying themselves on weekends. Few people will stop to buy lemonade on a rainy weekday morning. That's when many people are rushing to get to work.

The more people help, the faster the work goes.

Kids can learn to bake from their parents.

Some families like to bake together. It's a tasty way to work as a team. Adding homemade cookies and muffins to the lemonade stand can **boost** sales.

Everyone can help. Older children can read the recipe. Young bakers can mix and measure the ingredients. Adults can put the pans in the oven.

CHAPTER 3

Helping Other Families

Cats and dogs need food and water every day.

Many people have pets. They may need someone to check on their furry friends while they are at work or on vacation. Neighbors and friends can take turns caring for the pets. Dogs like to be walked and to spend time outside. Cats like to play.

Families can work together to make sure pets are cared for when their owners are away. Pets need attention and can't be left alone for too long. Families can spend time with the pets or bring them to their homes. If there is an emergency, families can take the animal to the vet. Together, the family can keep the pets fed, safe, and happy.

Some people have dog-walking businesses.

Playing on swings is a fun activity to enjoy with young children.

Babies and young children need a lot of attention. Families work together to take care of babies and young children. Older children look after their little brothers and sisters at home. They help get them washed and dressed. They read to them at bedtime.

Feeding a baby takes time.

Some families need extra help when they have small children. Babysitting is another way families work together. Babysitters take care of children while the grown-ups are away.

A babysitter goes by many names. Have you heard any of these terms?

> nanny
> child minder
> governess

> nurse
> au pair

Parents can go with their children to meet neighbors who want to **hire** a babysitter. Many hospitals offer classes for babysitters. The classes teach babysitters how to care for children and what to do in emergencies.

Babysitters can do many activities with children. They can do puzzles and play games together. They can play outside and work on craft projects.

Babysitters and kids like to read together.

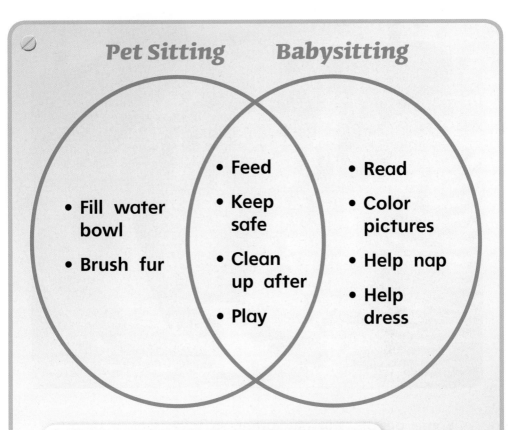

Pet Sitting **Babysitting**

- Fill water bowl
- Brush fur

- Feed
- Keep safe
- Clean up after
- Play

- Read
- Color pictures
- Help nap
- Help dress

This Venn diagram compares and contrasts pet sitting and babysitting.

Brothers and sisters who work together can do bigger jobs. There is outside work all year round. Children can work in teams to rake leaves in the fall. They can shovel snow in the winter. They can help plant gardens in the spring, and weed all summer. Some of these jobs are too big for one person to do alone. Working together as a family can get the job done faster.

Some people will pay others to wrap holiday gifts for them.

Families can start a small business together. The winter holiday is a perfect time to try a gift-wrapping business for friends and neighbors. All you need is wrapping paper, ribbons, and tape. Everyone can work together at a large table. There are many other ways families can work together. Can you think of some? Be creative!

Respond to Reading

Summarize

Use important details to summarize *Families at Work*.

Detail	Detail	Detail

Text Evidence

1. How do you know that *Families at Work* is expository text? Genre

2. How do babysitters care for children? Use details to support your answer Key Details

3. Use what you know about inflectional endings to figure out the meaning of *selling* on page 5. Inflectional Endings

4. What jobs can kids do to help others? Text to World

Compare Texts

Read to find out how a family in New Hampshire works together at a sawmill.

A Family Sawmill

Tina and her mother, Betty, work together at their sawmill in New Hampshire.

In 1975, George and Betty Woodell started a sawmill in New Hampshire. Sawmills are places where wood is cut into planks and boards for customers. Other sawmills had names that ended with "and Sons." George and Betty had two daughters, Tina and Tammy, so they called their sawmill Woodell and Daughters.

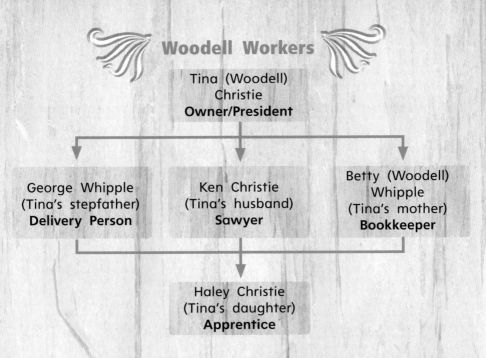

Woodell Workers

Tina (Woodell) Christie
Owner/President

George Whipple
(Tina's stepfather)
Delivery Person

Ken Christie
(Tina's husband)
Sawyer

Betty (Woodell) Whipple
(Tina's mother)
Bookkeeper

Haley Christie
(Tina's daughter)
Apprentice

Everyone has a role in a family business.

Learning the Business

Betty did not use a babysitter. Instead, she took Tina and Tammy with her to work.

The two sisters grew up around people cutting logs at the sawmill. The girls started their own small business as children. They sold firewood for 25 cents a box. Tina was older. She liked the sawmill more than her sister.

After **college**, Tina had a new job at the sawmill. She talked with customers and took their **orders**.

Tina's husband, Ken Christie, does a lot of the sawing.

When George Woodell passed away, Tina became the owner. Today, Woodell and Daughters is a strong business thanks to the help of family members. Tina's Uncle Scott worked at the sawmill for a while. Tina's mother still works there, and so does her new husband. Tina's husband works there, too. Now, Tina's daughter is growing up around a sawmill, just like her mother did. It's a real family business!

Make Connections

Why is it important for families to work together? ESSENTIAL QUESTION

How does the Woodell family work together like the families in *Families at Work*? TEXT TO TEXT

Glossary

actors *(AK-turz)* people who perform in movies or other shows *(page 2)*

boost *(BOOST)* to raise the amount of *(page 7)*

college *(KOL-ij)* a school attended after high school *(page 17)*

handyperson *(HAN-dee-PUR-suhn)* a person who fixes things around the house *(page 6)*

hire *(HIGHR)* to pay someone for their services or work *(page 12)*

orders *(OR-durz)* requests for goods or services *(page 17)*

schedule *(SKEJ-ool)* a day-by-day or hour-by-hour plan *(page 4)*

Index

Focus on
Social Studies

Purpose To find out how families you know work together

What to Do

Step 1 ▶ Ask your classmates how they work together with their families.

Step 2 ▶ Put your information in a chart like this one.

People	How They Help

Step 3 ▶ Compare and contrast how each family works together. Write about what you learned.